Lingo Dingo
and the
Russian chef

Written by Mark Pallis
Illustrated by James Cottell

For my awesome sons - MP

For Leo and Juniper - JC

LINGO DINGO AND THE RUSSIAN CHEF

All rights reserved. This book or any portion thereof may not be reproduced or used in any manner whatsoever without the express written permission of the publisher except for the use of brief excerpts in a review.

Story edited by Natascha Biebow, Blue Elephant Storyshaping
First Printing, 2022
ISBN: 978-1-915337-10-8
NeuWestendPress.com

Lingo Dingo
and the
Russian chef

Written by Mark Pallis
Illustrated by James Cottell

NEU WESTEND
— PRESS —

This is Lingo. She's a Dingo and she loves helping.
Anyone. Anytime. Anyhow.

Lingo often helps her stylish neighbour Gunther, who lives by himself next door. She does a few jobs and has a nice chat. It makes Gunter feel good and it makes Lingo feel good too.

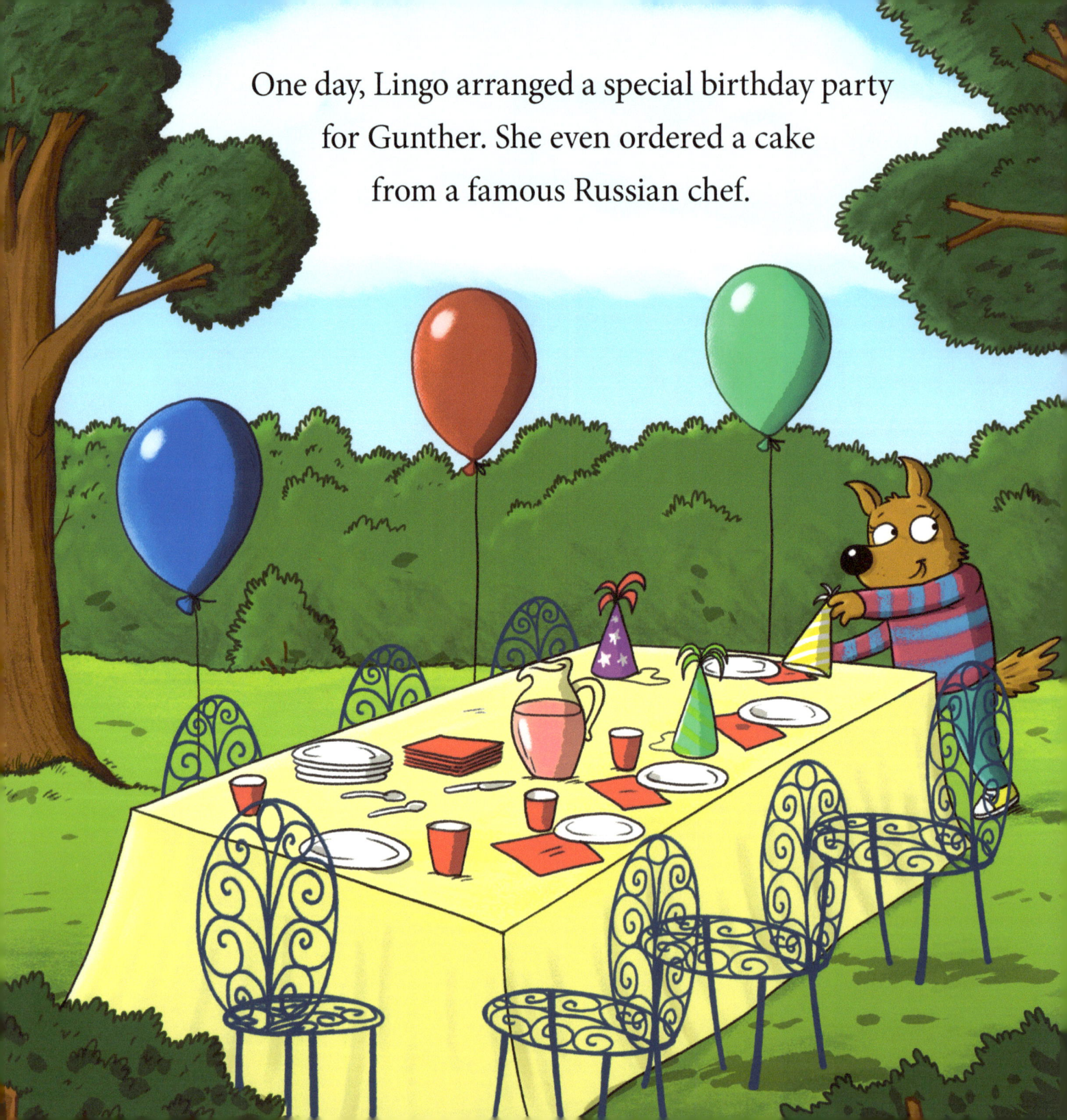

One day, Lingo arranged a special birthday party for Gunther. She even ordered a cake from a famous Russian chef.

There was a knock at the door, "It must be the cake!" said Lingo. But it was a monkey.

"Привет. Меня зовут Шеф Ноно. У меня проблема," he said.

Oh no. I can't speak Russian yet, thought Lingo. *Maybe 'Привет' is like 'Hello'.*

Привет = Hello; **Меня зовут** = My name is; **У меня проблема** = I have a problem.

"Привет," said Lingo. Chef Nono replied slowly,
Prosti. YA ne mogu ispech' tort ko dnyu rozhdeniya
"Прости. Я не могу испечь торт ко дню рождения."

"I don't understand," said Lingo. "But let me guess. You want..."

Прости = I am sorry; **торт ко дню рождения** = birthday cake
Я не могу испечь торт ко дню рождения = I cannot make the birthday cake

Moya dukhovka slomalas
"Моя духовка сломалась," explained Chef.
Mogu ya vospol'zovat'sya tvoyey dukhovkoy
"Могу я воспользоваться твоей духовкой?"

Chef's oven must be broken thought Lingo. "I know! Let's bake the cake together," she said.

Моя духовка = my oven; **сломалась** = is broken;
Могу я = can I; **Могу я воспользоваться твоей духовкой** = can I use your oven

Chef Nono and Lingo whizzed around the kitchen:

Вот тебе фартук = here is your apron; **Венчик** = a whisk
Миска для смешивания = a mixing bowl

"Передай мне масло, сахар, яйца и муку, пожалуйста," said Chef.

Lingo wasn't sure what those words meant, so she just grabbed fish, coffee and onions instead.

"Рыба, кофе и лук. Гадость," laughed Chef.

Передай мне = pass me; **масло** = butter; **сахар** = sugar; **яйца** = eggs; **и** = and; **муку** = flour; **пожалуйста** = please; **Рыба** = fish; **кофе** = coffee; **лук** = onions; **Гадость** = disgusting

Chef plopped butter, sugar, eggs and flour into a bowl. "So that's what 'масло, сахар, яйца и муку' means!" laughed Lingo.

<small>maslo, sakhar, yaytsa i muku</small>

<small>YA smeshivayu, ty smeshivayesh', my smeshivayem</small>

"Я смешиваю, ты смешиваешь, мы смешиваем," said Chef and together they began to mix the cake.

Я смешиваю = I mix; **ты смешиваешь** = you mix; **мы смешиваем** = we mix

^{Nakonets, razrykhlitel'. Dve lozhki}
"Наконец, разрыхлитель. Две ложки," said Chef. Lingo guessed 'разрыхлитель' meant baking powder, but how much?

Before she could ask, Chef hurried away, saying,
^{Izvini, mne nuzhno sdelat' pi-pi}
"Извини, мне нужно сделать пи-пи."

Lingo laughed, "I can guess what 'пи-пи' means!"

Наконец = finally; **разрыхлитель** = baking powder; **Две ложки** = two spoonfulls; **Извини** = excuse me; **мне нужно сделать пи-пи** = I need to do a wee wee

I wonder if this is too much? thought Lingo as she added ten spoonfulls of 'разрыхлитель' to the mix.

She carefully put everything into the oven and before long, a sweet cakey smell filled the kitchen.

разрыхлитель = baking powder

Chto sluchilos'? Ono ogromnoye
"Что случилось? Оно огромное!" said Chef.

Lingo realised she had added too much baking powder.
"Sorry," she said sheepishly.

Что случилось = what happened; **Оно огромное** = it is huge

Катастрофа = disaster

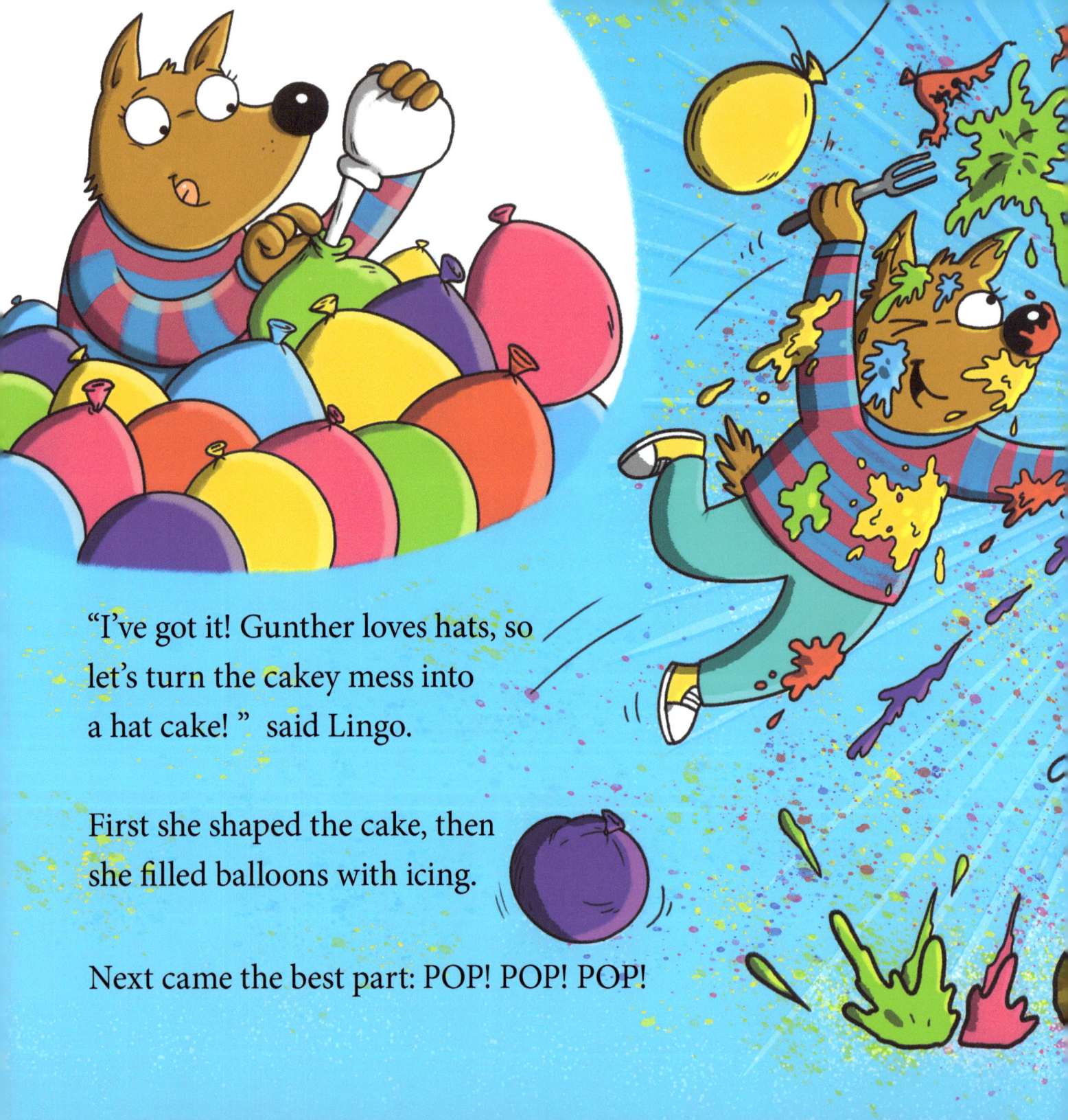

"I've got it! Gunther loves hats, so let's turn the cakey mess into a hat cake!" said Lingo.

First she shaped the cake, then she filled balloons with icing.

Next came the best part: POP! POP! POP!

It was a messy job but in the end, the cake looked fantastic. "Красный, оранжевый, желтый, зеленый, синий. Фантастика!" said Chef.
Krasnyy, oranzhevyy, zheltyy, zelenyy, siniy. Fantastika

Красный = red; **оранжевый** = orange; **желтый** = yellow; **зеленый** = green; **синий** = blue; **Фантастика** = fantastic

There was a knock at the door.
"Дверь!" said Chef.
(Dver')
It was Gunther, and he was wearing his special hat!

"Thank you. This makes me feel so special," said Gunther. "You are special," replied Lingo.

Дверь = the door

Gunter was thrilled with his cake.
Chef's deep voice sang "С Днем рождения тебя ..."
S Dnem rozhdeniya tebya

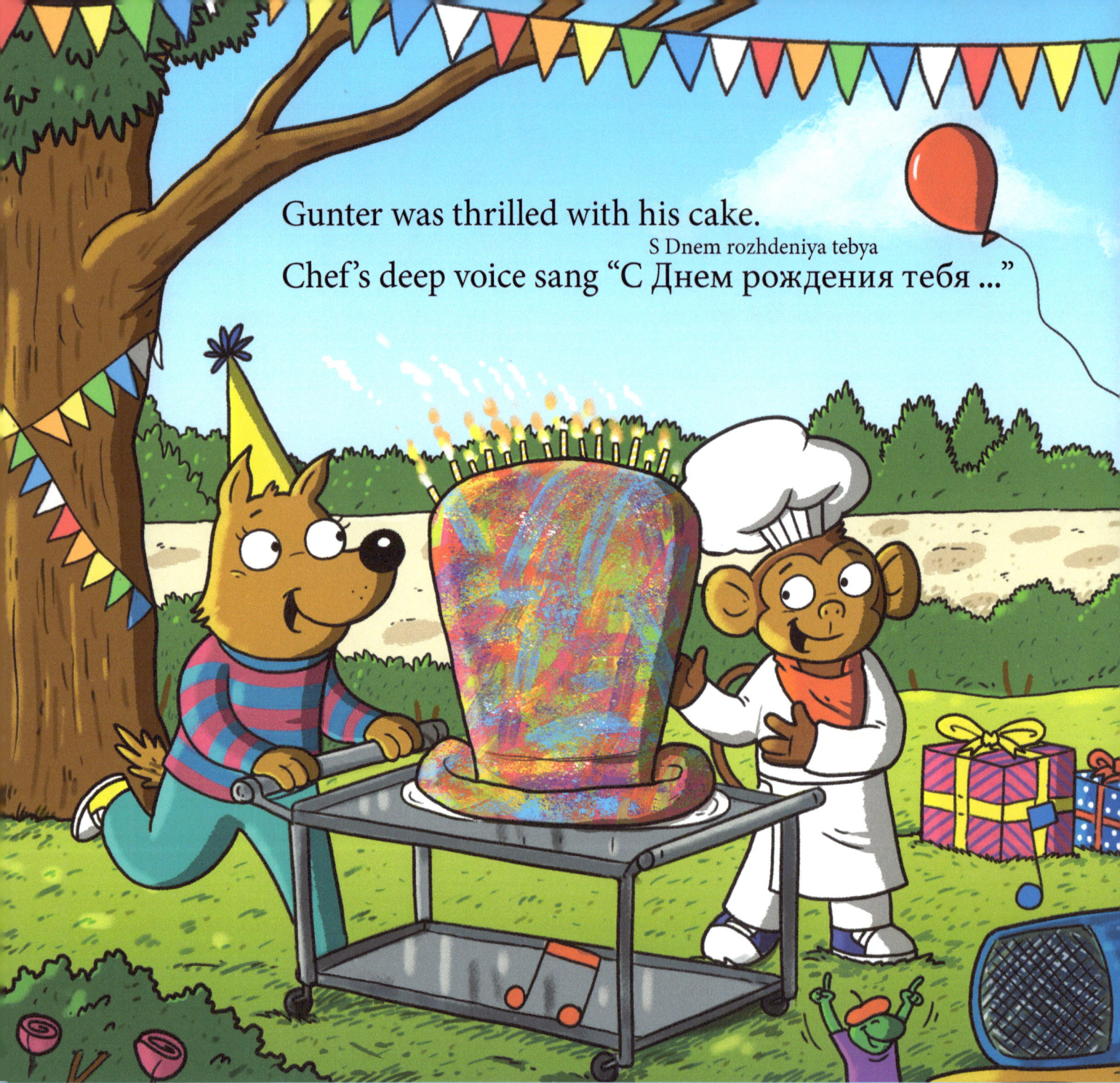

С Днем рождения тебя = Happy birthday to you

"дуть!" said Chef.

Gunther blew out all the candles in one puff and everyone tucked in.

дуть = blow

Everyone was happy.
"YA schastliv
Я счастлив,
ty schastliva
ты счастлива.
My vse schastlivy
Мы все счастливы," cheered Chef.

Я счастлив = I am happy; **ты счастлива** = you are happy;
Мы все счастливы = we are all happy;

Baking a cake, helping a friend, learning a new language ... what a day!

But now it was time for bed. It was time to dream about all the fun things that might happen tomorrow.

Learning to love languages

An additional language opens a child's mind, broadens their horizons and enriches their emotional life. Research has shown that the time between a child's birth and their sixth or seventh birthday is a "golden period" when they are most receptive to new languages. This is because they have an in-built ability to distinguish the sounds they hear and make sense of them. The Story-powered Language Learning Method taps into these natural abilities.

How the Story-powered language learning Method works

We create an emotionally engaging and funny story for children and adults to enjoy together, just like any other picture book. Studies show that social interaction, like enjoying a book together, is critical in language learning.

Through the story, we introduce a relatable character who speaks only in the new language. This helps build empathy and a positive attitude towards people who speak different languages. These are both important aspects in laying the foundations for lasting language acquisition in a child's life.

As the story progresses, the child naturally works with the characters to discover the meanings of a wide range of fun new words. Strategic use of humour ensures that this subconscious learning is rewarded with laughter; the child feels good and the first seeds of a lifelong love of languages are sown.

OVER 50 languages now available! From French to Polish, and MANY MORE!
www.neuwestendpress.com

You can learn more words and phrases with these hilarious, heartwarming stories from NEU WESTEND PRESS

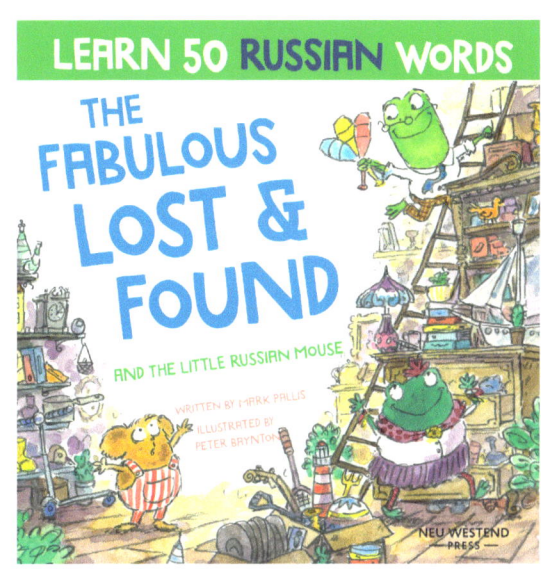

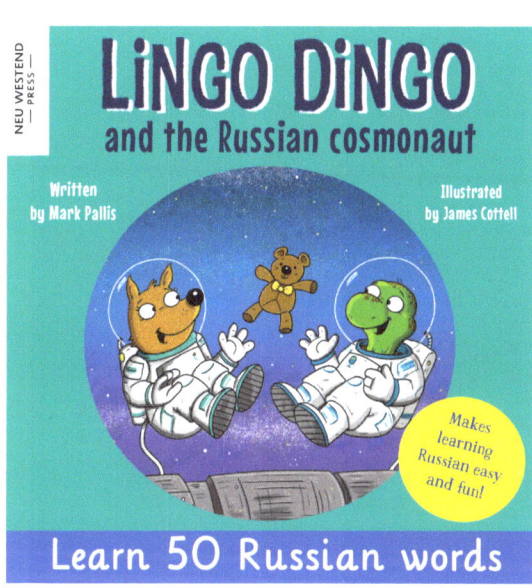

@MARK_PALLIS on twitter
www.neuwestendpress.com

To download your FREE certifcate, and more cool stuff, visit
www.neuwestendpress.com

@jamescottell on INSTAGRAM
www.jamescottellstudios.co.uk

"I want people to be so busy laughing, they don't realise they're learning!"

Mark Pallis

Crab and Whale is the bestselling story of how a little Crab helps a big Whale. It's carefully designed to help even the most energetic children find a moment of calm and focus. It also includes a special mindful breathing exercise and affirmation for children.

Featured as one of Mindful.org's 'Seven Mindful Children's books'

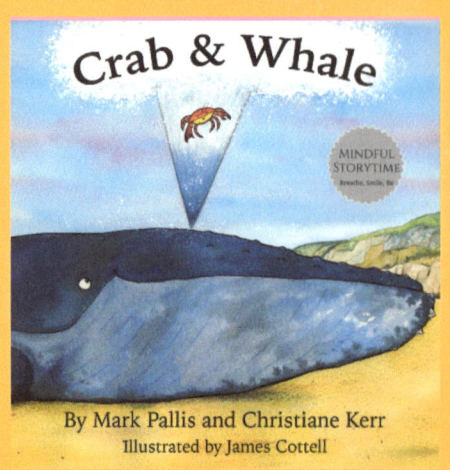

Do you call them hugs or cuddles?

In this funny, heartwarming rhyming story, you will laugh out loud as two loveable gibbons try to figure out if a hug is better than a cuddle and, in the process, learn how to get along.

A perfect story for anyone who loves a hug (or a cuddle!)

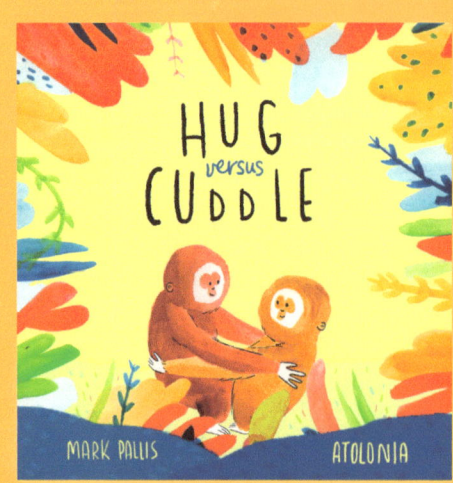

www.markpallis.com

www.ingramcontent.com/pod-product-compliance
Lightning Source LLC
Chambersburg PA
CBHW041126130526
44590CB00054B/45